PRESENTATION

*To* _____

*From* _____

*Date* _____

# CHRIST'S KEYS TO HAPPINESS

---

## BY GEORGE W. BARRETT

---

WORLD INSPIRATIONAL BOOKS

*an ORIGINAL*

*Edited by*

DAVID A. MacLENNAN

---

THE WORLD PUBLISHING COMPANY

NEW YORK AND CLEVELAND

# ACKNOWLEDGMENTS

Acknowledgment is gratefully made to the following publishers for the use of copyright material.

NATIONAL COUNCIL OF THE CHURCHES OF CHRIST in the U. S. A.
For scripture quotations designated R.S.V. from the *REVISED STANDARD VERSION BIBLE,* copyright 1946 and 1952 by the Division of Christian Education of the National Council of the Churches of Christ in the U. S. A.

OXFORD AND CAMBRIDGE UNIVERSITY PRESSES
For scripture passages designated N.E.B. from *The New English Bible,* © The Delegates of The Oxford University Press and The Syndics of The Cambridge University Press 1961, 1970.

Published by The World Publishing Company
Published simultaneously in Canada
by Nelson, Foster & Scott Ltd.

First printing—1970

**WORLD PUBLISHING**
**TIMES MIRROR**
NEW YORK AND CLEVELAND

# CONTENTS

*To the memory of my parents*
*who faced truth openly and courageously*

# INTRODUCTION

THIS IS a rare book. It is rare in the sense that it sheds light upon the Beatitudes of Jesus as no other book on the theme known to the editor of this series. Dr. George W. Barrett, the author, with uncommon and penetrating insight into the mind of Christ, writes of the words of one whom millions call Lord and Saviour, and of our human situation. He links the seven sayings of Jesus on the cross with the Beatitudes in searching fashion, and with a relevance to the age of affluence, of assassinations and other expressions of human violence, and of the proud achievements of the Space Age. At times you will feel that your mind and conscience have been "stabbed broad awake." Nevertheless, the deep comfort of the Gospel of Christ is mediated through the words of the author. *Christ's Keys to Happiness* will open new doors to understanding the profound joy of which Christ spoke and which he communicates to all who realize his presence as our eternal contemporary. As Dr. Barrett writes of the sayings of Jesus on "Two Hills," the thoughtful reader will understand the Beatitudes "in an unusual, profound and, in the best sense of that word, sophisticated way."

The author realizes his purpose: "to show how the man who spoke so confidently of strange kinds of blessedness and joy upon a peaceful hill in Palestine also spoke with similar confidence as he died in pain and darkness."

# ABOUT THE AUTHOR

GEORGE W. BARRETT, until recently Bishop of the Episcopal Diocese of Rochester, New York, was born in Iowa City, Iowa. At an early age he moved with his family to California. He is a graduate of the University of California at Los Angeles, and of the Episcopal Theological School, Cambridge, Massachusetts, from which he gained the degree of Bachelor of Divinity. After beginning his career as assistant minister of St. Paul's Church, Oakland, California he became rector of St. Mark's Church, Upland, and chaplain to Episcopal students of Pomona College, Scripps College, and Claremont College, in what he naturally regarded as his home state. Subsequently he served as rector of St. Luke's Church, Monrovia, and as rector of St. James' Church, Los Angeles (1947–52). In 1952 he accepted the call of General Theological Seminary, New York City, to become professor of pastoral theology. A most effective preacher and pastor himself, he taught candidates for the ministry how to communicate the Gospel and exercise "the cure (or care) of souls" entrusted to them as pastors. In 1955 he became rector of Christ Church, Bronxville, New York. From this parish he was elected Bishop of Rochester, New York, in 1963. He resigned the episcopate for personal reasons on January 1, 1970, and entered the consulting field. He is author of *Key Words for Lent* and of *Demands on Ministry Today: The Issue of Integrity,* both published by Seabury Press.

The editor of this series knew and admired him during his Rochester ministry, and because of Dr. Barrett's sense of the great Church embracing all Christians, considered him as did many of every branch of Christianity as "everybody's bishop." He was a loyal churchman in the best sense of that phrase—ecumenical, public-spirited, and willing to give costly service on behalf of all for whom Christ died and rose again. He is now and will remain a man committed to Christ and to the Church, a realist about human nature and society, but, to borrow a phrase from the late great theologian Paul Tillich, a "belief-ful realist." George W. Barrett presently resides in San Francisco.

—David A. MacLennan
*General Editor*

# FOREWORD

O NE SIGN of the largeness and wholeness of the story of Jesus and the person of Christ is the way in which people make part of the story and separate aspects of the man seem whole and plausible in themselves. Thus Christ is presented convincingly as a teacher, a prophet, a healer, a revolutionary, and a saviour. There may be value in so pinpointing part of the truth, but there is great danger, too, in holding out parts as if any one of them were the whole.

The purpose of this book is to show the wholeness of Christ by relating the Beatitudes which he spoke near the beginning of his ministry to the words attributed to him as he died on the cross. Jesus as teacher and Jesus as the Saviour, sacrificing his life for others in mysterious fulfillment of God's will, are often pictured in ways that suggest two different characters, with separate aims and outlooks, appealing to different kinds of people and speaking to different human needs. But we shall see that the same Christ fulfills both roles in a remarkably unified manner.

I am grateful to all who have shared in the creation of this book—to David MacLennan for asking me to write it as well as for his outstanding example as a preacher and interpreter of Christ; to my wife, Bettina, for her suggestions, help, and the use of her poems on the burial of Martin Luther King and the "Way of the Cross," as well as her share in typing the manuscript; and to Mrs. Thomas C. T. Buckley, who also helped produce the manuscript at various stages of its development and typed the final draft for publication. Chiefly I am thankful for the responsiveness and encouragement of the people of the many congregations to whom I have preached and to whom I have sought, particularly on Good Fridays, to interpret the cross in relation to the entire event of Christ and its meaning for our time.

George W. Barrett

# I

# WORDS FROM TWO HILLS

ST. MATTHEW 5:1    *"When he saw the crowds, he went up the hill. There he took his seat, and when his disciples had gathered around him he began to address them." (N.E.B.)*

ST. JOHN 19:18    *"There they crucified him, and with him two others, one on either side and Jesus between them." (R.S.V.)*

ST. MATTHEW 5:10    *"Blessed are those who are persecuted for righteousness' sake for theirs is the kingdom of heaven." (R.S.V.)*

N OT GOOD if detached" is a warning sometimes printed on bus or railroad tickets, or on season tickets to plays and concerts. In this way you are reminded that you must buy the whole package in order to enjoy any of its contents.

Many of the words of Jesus fall into such a category, for much of his teaching means little if it is isolated from the rest of what he said, from the life he lived, and from the meaning of that life as understood by those who came in contact with him. Some of his words are grossly misleading if they are read all by themselves as, for example, his rather chilling warning, "If anyone comes to me and does not hate his own father and mother and wife and children and brothers and sisters, yes, and even his own life, he cannot be my disciple." Imagination, sensitivity, and some knowledge of Near Eastern hyperbole are required to read this saying as a demand for commitment so intense as to make ordinary ties seem hatred by comparison.

Not even the familiar Golden Rule, "Whatever you wish that men should do to you, so do to them," or the two Great Commandments from the Old Testament upon which our Lord said the whole Law depended, "You shall love the Lord your God with all your heart and with all your mind and with all your strength," and "You shall love your neighbor as yourself," stand alone. Treating others as you would like to be treated may do others more harm than good unless your desires for yourself are healthful. Loving your neighbor as yourself is destructive if you love yourself in the wrong way, or if you try to express love to your neighbor while carrying around a load of unrecognized self-hatred. And how does one love God without some convictions of the nature and character of God? What sort of actions demonstrate human love toward him?

People sometimes think of the Sermon on the Mount as standing alone as a compilation of the ethical teachings of Jesus. Compilation the Sermon certainly is, a gathering up of teachings given by him at various times and places, but even this compilation is neither self-explanatory nor self-validating as anyone knows who has tried to understand it, much less live it. Nor are the well-known Beatitudes with which the Sermon begins obvious or self-evident, even though a famous educator once tried to link the separate Beatitudes to character traits desirable in measuring the moral and emotional growth of children.

It seems incredible that anyone ever should have considered the Beatitudes a success story. Is a man well adjusted to society when he is persecuted for righteousness' sake? Is poverty of goods desirable in an affluent society, or poverty of spirit in a competitive one? Do the merciful obtain mercy or are they despised and tramped upon for their compassion?

There is little evidence of the meek inheriting the earth. Those who mourn are sometimes comforted; often sorrow brings bitterness and despair. Those who passionately hunger and thirst for righteousness frequently remain unsatisfied, their search ending in self-accusing scrupulosity or insufferable pride. Purity of heart is interpreted in terms of deliverance from the passionate joys of the flesh. Everyone pays lip service to peace and peacemaking, but sociologists stress the need of open conflict and demonstrate the destructive effects of the lack of such waged by the poor and the black, between husbands and wives, parents and children, friend and friend. To rejoice when you are reviled and persecuted can give rise to a well-founded suspicion that you are priggishly self-righteous, even a bit paranoid.

Surely the Beatitudes need to be understood in an unusual, profound, and, in the best sense of that word, sophisticated way if they are to be accepted as describing the attitude and conduct that make for blessedness and joy. Living by them can be dangerous living indeed. We easily overlook this fact, for the Beatitudes have gathered to themselves all the sentimental associations connected with the allegedly simple teachings of an idyllic country preacher who went about doing good, while the truth is that he who taught the Beatitudes died because of the way he lived and for what he taught. His own warning is plain enough. "Blessed are those who are persecuted for righteousness' sake, for theirs is the kingdom of heaven." His words were fulfilled when he was crucified between two thieves.

Far from being a standard upon which a society is soundly created and successfully maintained, the Beatitudes could very nearly be regarded as a prescription for tearing it down by removing the incentives upon which it is built. Leadership of a nation does not come from the meek, or the poor in spirit, or the mournful, or those overscrupulous about righteousness in achieving their ends. Few nations survive without either the power to make war or the protection of strong neighbors ready for battle. A stable society is built upon confidence and respect, not on persecution of the righteous, or lies told about the godly.

Small wonder that the earliest Christians were accused of turning the world upside down, those people whose faith flowed from the scandal and folly of a crucified and defeated leader. If then we honestly consider the Beatitudes, we must do so in the light of the cross and see their teaching fulfilled by the cross.

This, too, is dangerous, for just as it is easy to sentimentalize the Beatitudes, so it is easy to sentimentalize and glamorize the cross, using it as an ornament in churches and as jewelry to be hung around our necks. The danger goes deeper than that. We are inclined to weep nostalgic tears over what happened to a man two thousand years ago and use that very memory to escape similar confrontations today. After Martin Luther King was assassinated just before Holy Week of 1968, an angry man said to me, "I doubt that the churches are making any real effort to meet the sickness and the crises that confront this nation and the world. You can tell that by looking at their plans for Good Friday. They are planning to talk and sing about the seven last words of Christ on the cross just as they always have done rather than facing the issues that are tearing our society apart."

I remember being moved by his urgency and being disturbed by his implication that there is no connection between the story of the cross and what is happening around us today, no connection between the cross and the nuclear arms race or the ABM, between poverty and ghettos, black anger and white backlash, inadequate welfare and substandard housing, the agony of Vietnam and the Middle East, Nigeria and Biafra, South Africa and

Rhodesia. I continue to be disturbed by his fear that we preach about the cross and do not speak to our present condition, that we should talk of the words of Christ on the cross without showing them to be words of life, hope, and healing.

In all the centuries of Christian history more Good Fridays than not have come in times of crises and war, plague, famine, and disaster in some part of the world. And this day always holds in front of our eyes disturbing and terrifying facts about ourselves as well as an amazing and glorious picture of the God whom we worship. The cross is the most characteristic symbol of our faith, for the man on the cross shows the length and depth of God's love for mankind and demonstrates the manner in which we respond to that love, the ways in which we accept it or refuse it.

On Good Friday we know that Christmas Christianity by itself is insufficient. "Peace on earth, goodwill toward men" fails to express the fullness of the faith we profess unless its peace is found on the far side of the cross and its goodwill the will of men whose pride has been broken by the same cross. The good news of great joy will be as old and dated as yesterday's newspaper unless it is tidings of a joy that can face rejection and pass through death. And only those who have been to the cross can safely approach the manger, for even the festal Mass of Christmas continues to be a commemoration of a death and resurrection.

Our religion is more than following a man who went around doing good. For his goodness was shockingly offensive to the virtue of this world. Even his chosen disciples followed him only at a safe distance and deserted him at the end. The three men on the crosses at the place called The Skull had much in common. All of them were being punished by their fellow men and by the law of the state but for vastly different reasons.

The thieves represent those who cannot get along with others because they live by preying on others, because their standards are lower than the accepted standards of honest and decent men. They are too dangerous to be permitted to remain at large and there are those who say, mistakenly I am sure, that some of them are too dangerous to be permitted to continue living at all. There lurk in almost every man and woman latent criminal tendencies, a deep streak of violence, something of the avariciousness that tries to snatch more from life than we are willing to put into it. Most men, most of the time, are smart enough, even virtuous enough, to control such inclinations, at least enough to get by as far as the law or friends or the public are concerned. But when a crisis comes we find a man who tramples his way to safety in the earthquake rubble or from the sinking ship, the looter or the hoarder in a disaster-ridden city, the rumormonger who spreads panic by gossip in a riot-torn community, the soldier who shoots down helpless civilians, even women and children, in vengeful, sadistic rage, the man who loses control over his emotions in a personal relationship. In recent·years this whole nation has felt guilty for acts of violence and assassination, and uneasy about the war in Vietnam, not so much because we actually knew or believed ourselves guilty, but because these events made us aware of the strength and persistence of violence in our national character, of how prone we are to seek our own way regardless of the cost to others. When we are caught and punished under such circumstances, we receive the reward of our deeds, often with unjustly compounded interest, for guilty men try to get rid of their guilt by looking for scapegoats and showing vengeance toward those whom they believe more guilty than themselves.

However, we are more concerned with the central cross. Our Lord represents those who are punished not because they are worse than ordinary men but so much better that ordinary men feel threatened by them, ignore them, ridicule them, even refuse to live in the same world with them.

We shall not find it difficult, then, to trace a connection between the seven sayings of Jesus on the cross and the Beatitudes with which he began the Sermon on the Mount, a connection demonstrating that the kind of character described in the Sermon on the Mount is no guaranty for success, no sage advice on how to win your way and have people like you. Instead, the Beatitudes describe a character who can easily be lead to the cross and can be understood only in the light of the cross. How could it be otherwise when the man who lived by the Beatitudes died because of the way he lived? The closer we come to living by the Beatitudes the more risk we run of finding ourselves nailed to a cross.

"Blessed are those who are persecuted for righteousness' sake for theirs is the kingdom of heaven." His being persecuted and his calling blessed those who are persecuted for righteousness' sake show that the world will not put up with too much righteousness. In the play *Billy Budd,* adapted from Melville's novel, there is a sentence, "Life takes its revenge on those who have hurt its pride with innocence." We do tend to suspect and deride any unusual sort of innocence or virtue, even that shown by the teacher, the nurse, or the office worker demonstrating more concern or compassion for student or patient or the public than do fellow workers and thereby threatening them. Good people were so threatened by the presence of Christ. He said that he had come not to judge but to save the world. The world judged itself by its response to him.

The cross continues as a judgment, particularly upon our standards of success. To be successful, your achievements must stand out from the crowd and still be the sort that the crowd recognizes as its own. People seek leaders like themselves, men with whom they can identify. They are inclined to fear leaders too much stronger than themselves. Above all they fear leaders who dare to flout the conventional assumptions of the moment or the age, when most people are taking them for granted, assumptions such as slavery or discrimination, the assumption of the affluent or near affluent that those on welfare are always slothful or that poverty must always continue, the assumption that the piling up of a balance of terror is a safe way to peace.

"Blessed are those who are persecuted for righteousness' sake. . . . Woe to you when all men speak well of you." These are dangerous observations, for they easily lead to a feckless fanaticism that mistakes folly for wisdom, untactless stubbornness for heroism, and insensitivity for the defense of the Gospel. No one will deny that popular people, the obviously successful people, are needed and valuable in every community.

The astronauts are examples of this. The moon landings have been called a triumph of the squares, a victory for middle America. The astronauts were brave men, unselfishly working together, imaginatively yet meticulously going about their enterprise, risking their lives in a matter-of-fact, unheroic way that was indeed heroic. They embodied a kind of goodness and a solidity of character that represent the best traditions of their country and echo the aspirations of their fellow citizens.

There are times when even prophetic leadership is applauded, when a Savonarola will dominate Florence before that city turns against him, or when the voice of a President will lift a nation to new heights of vision and new courses of action, when men like Franklin Roosevelt and the Kennedys will have the gift of speaking their convictions strongly, of influencing many different kinds of people and at least for a while carrying majorities with them. The assassinations of the Kennedy brothers were freak actions rather than popular rejections. We are not required to seek either success or martyrdom, but rather to be faithful and accept either one, even the cross of not having a cross without feeling guilt about that either. Still it is true that many of our richest blessings, many of mankind's most significant forward steps, have come through those who have been rejected by their contemporaries, by those who have been persecuted for righteousness' sake, who in some measure have shared the isolation of the central cross on Calvary.

Such rejection and persecution do not always come through bullets and violence. They also come through being ignored. Indeed, indifference is more the opposite of love than is hate. Or they may consist in being misunderstood and ridiculed as almost every great President of this nation and many lesser ones have been. Often the answer to such abuse can be nothing but silence like that of our Lord before Pilate or upon the cross, silence in the hope of history's vindication. Even the verdict of history is uncertain and untrustworthy for historians endlessly debate the significance of past events while controversies continue for decades and centuries about the motives, the characters, or the competence of leaders of the past. Abraham Lincoln was ridiculed and vilified by many of his contemporaries. Later generations canonized him. At present some suspect and denigrate him on the ridiculously anachronistic ground that he did not possess a whole century ago views on integration and black power appropriate to the 1960's. He spoke of firmness in the right as God gives us to see the right. Beyond silence in the hope of history's vindication is the silence of faith in God's vindication, knowing that in the end he will reveal things as they are.

In such faith Jesus said, "Blessed are those who are persecuted for right-eousness' sake for theirs is the kingdom of heaven." Almost all his teaching was conditioned by his convictions about that kingdom. By "kingdom of heaven" we mean the kingdom or the rule of God on earth rather than life in a realm beyond death. Jesus began his ministry by saying, "The time is fulfilled and the kingdom of God is at hand; repent and believe in the Gospel." (Mark 1:15 R.S.V.) He believed that God was about to act in a new and decisive way, about to establish a reign of love and justice, joy and peace. Because this kingdom was at hand men were to repent, change their ways, and believe the good news. The Beatitudes are a way of describing how a citizen of that kingdom will behave while God is establishing it. He will live confidently and courageously without anxiety about material riches, wait-ing in hope, knowing that he will be an inheritor of the riches of that kingdom, passionately seeking its righteousness as he would the choicest food and drink, with a purity and a sensitivity that enable him to see the signs of God acting, mediating the peace of that kingdom as a child of God. He will even accept with joy whatever misunderstanding and persecution come at a time of transition from one order to another, with standards and values changing and the entire shape of things turned upside down.

It all sounds rather naive put in this way, for the kingdom did not come in the way Jesus seemed to think it would. It has not yet come in any fullness, although when men have tried to live by its standards they have known at least a foretaste and a foreshadowing of its reality. Perhaps it is just as well that our Lord had such confidence in the kingdom that he underestimated the time it would take to establish it. For now the Beatitudes, rather than being a code of conduct applicable only to first-century Christians, become the impossible standard toward which we strive and by which we seek to live. They may be impossible to follow literally, but they can always be taken seriously.

So the Beatitudes were always more than good advice. From the first they were a part of the good news of a new kingdom. Later they were proclaimed in the name of a living Lord by a Church that remembered his death and resurrection and that related them both to his suffering and to his victory.

We are considering here the Beatitudes in the context of the cross. We shall show how the man who spoke so confidently of strange kinds of blessedness and joy upon a peaceful hill in Palestine also spoke with similar confidence as he died in pain and darkness. And it will be an empty cross in the end, for with those who first recorded the Beatitudes we no longer consider ourselves disciples of a human Jesus speaking from mountains, walking the roads of Galilee, rejected and done to death, but as witnesses of a victorious Lord who had passed through death, the Son of a God who will not be put out of history, a Christ who is the clue to the meaning of life itself and whose assurances of the kingdom will in the end be completely fulfilled. Because of this we can live in some measure as citizens of that kingdom, even in a world of continued sin and imperfection, as men both of misery and of dignity.

After proclaiming, "Blessed are those who are persecuted for righteousness' sake for theirs is the kingdom of heaven," Jesus turned to his disciples and said, "How blessed are you when you suffer insults and persecution and every kind of calumny for my sake. Accept it with gladness and exaltation, for you have a rich reward in heaven; in the same way they persecuted the prophets before you." (Matthew 5:11 N.E.B.)

Perhaps recalling these words, certainly remembering the cross, the author of the Epistle to the Hebrews urges us to "run with resolution the race for which we are entered, our eyes fixed on Jesus, on whom faith depends from start to finish: Jesus who, for the sake of the joy that lay ahead of him, endured the cross, making light of its disgrace, and has taken his seat at the right hand of the throne of God." (Hebrews 12:1,2 N.E.B.)

# THE PEACE OF PARDON

St. Luke 23:34     *"And Jesus said, 'Father, forgive them; for they know not what they do.'" (R.S.V.)*

St. Matthew 5:9     *"Blessed are the peacemakers: for they shall be called the children of God." (K.J.V.)*

I<small>T</small> is almost always hard to forgive; hard to forgive oneself and hard to forgive others. It is hard to forgive acts that have caused deep hurt, or inflicted sharp pain. It is hard to forgive neglect of duty, or failure to act in time to prevent great damage to a child, to an invalid, or to society. It is this last sort of failure that is plaguing our country today, as we reap the harvest of neglect in decaying cities, polluted countryside and angry conflicts.

Sometimes a man will say, "I will never forgive him for that." This indicates that while we will forgive the ordinary mistakes and the common faults, there are limits beyond which no pardon is possible. No one who has lived through the recent generations can forget certain terrible actions in some parts of the world for which there seems to be no possibility for forgiveness. I recall an exhibit of pictures made by children in a concentration camp in Czechoslovakia some twenty-five years ago. They were shown in a synagogue in the belief that the memory of those days must never be forgotten. One reads of the trials of Nazi war criminals apprehended and arrested for deeds they allegedly committed more than a quarter of a century ago. People change much in twenty-five years and it may seem cruel and vengeful to try old men for offenses they committed during the fever of war and under the contagion of a spirit that infected an order long since crumbled. But then one realizes the need to keep alive the memory of the depths to which men can sink under such circumstances. For no people are really immune to such infection. One of the more disturbing things about the war in Vietnam is the knowledge that without any ruthless philosophy of a master race and often with the best of intentions we are committing at least some of the deeds for which we condemned the Nazis, such as attacks on civilians and uprooting, even killing, innocent people and burning their villages. Many Americans cannot forgive themselves for this, although they may have had no direct part in it and protest against it.

Perhaps the meaning of our present unrest in America is that many black Americans have reached the limit of their capacity to forgive in the face of repeated betrayal and disappointment.

Many of us know people who were once our friends, but now between us a thick wall of alienation has grown, a wall that we have no desire to tear down. We will forgive, we say, but we cannot forget. But we say this in a way indicating we have not really forgiven. Forgiveness obviously does not and cannot demand forgetting, but it requires loving acceptance in spite of remembering. We may know people who have never forgiven us and there is nothing we can do about it. Some have former wives or husbands from whom they have been separated in unforgiving alienation, parents and children who will never enter one another's houses.

Jesus said, "Father forgive them for they know not what they do." (Luke 23:34 K.J.V.) He was asking pardon for offenses of which his enemies were not even aware.

Forgiveness usually can be managed if the offender realizes his fault, when he genuinely apologizes and makes an honest attempt at restitution. If someone comes to you and says, "I am very sorry for the things I said," or, "I regret very much what I did," you rarely can hold out. You may mistrust him but your anger melts, for it is almost impossible to hold a grudge against one who is genuinely sorry. You may not like him or respect him, but you cease hating him. Likewise we know that if we go to a person whom we have wronged and ask his pardon, there is every likelihood that he will grant it.

It is different and much harder to forgive people who are utterly unaware of having done anything wrong at all. How do you establish trust with someone who looks at life so differently than you do, who lives in a world so different from your world that you behave very differently, each of you believing that your way is the right way? Sin is much deeper than missing the mark that we know is there. It is often a matter of failing to see the mark at all, or aiming at the wrong target.

Jesus asked forgiveness for the soldiers who carried out their orders, no doubt confident that they were doing their duty when they nailed him to the cross. He was asking forgiveness for the perverted virtues of his enemies, fairly good men who thought that they were doing the right thing. The deepest sin is almost always unconscious, not conscious. Far more dangerous than a child's deliberate defiance of his parents are the cruelties of children to children in the otherwise good gang life of which they are a part. The tragedy of Vietnam, like the tragedy of most wars, lies in the fact that the men on both sides unselfishly sacrifice for what they believe to be right. The zeal of our brave men is matched by the zeal and bravery of the Viet Cong and the armies of North Vietnam. One can have all kinds of doubts about our policy there, but few doubts of the patriotism and high character of most of those who represent us there. From the seedbed of honest segregationist sentiment springs the violence of a fanatic, and such violence finds its response in the desperate acts of those who sincerely believe that violence alone will advance the cause of justice for the black man.

Human failure has been compared to an iceberg adrift in the ocean. A very small part of the iceberg rises above the water and can be seen by navigators. This visible part of the iceberg is like the conscious faults, the visible perils that we can see and avoid or, if we hit them once, we still may be fortunate enough to reach harbor, repair the damage through repentance, and be more careful another time.

But much more of an iceberg lies below the surface, invisible from above. So the *Titanic,* already going too fast in dangerous waters, veered off to the side of the sighted iceberg. The officers on the bridge thought they had missed it at the very moment the jagged ice below the waterline ripped open the whole side of the vessel and doomed her to destruction.

So there are the offenses of which we are never conscious, the things we never meant to say, but did, or having said them had no idea of the hurt they caused, or of the things we should have said or done and were not alert enough to. We might have avoided some of this trouble had we not been traveling so selfishly or carelessly, ignoring repeated warnings of danger, as our society has been doing for more than a decade. Some trouble we never could have escaped anyway, for with the best of goodwill there are the inevitable hazards and the ambiguous choices of living in an imperfect world.

Life is so full of such perils that we literally know not what we do. Dietrich Bonhoeffer saw this and wrote in his *Prisoner for God,* "Folly is a more dangerous enemy to the good than malice. You can protest against malice, you can unmask it or prevent it by force. Malice always contains the seeds of its own destruction for it makes men uncomfortable if nothing worse. There is no defense against folly." *

He states that the fool cannot be saved by education, but that "the only cure for folly is spiritual redemption, for that alone can enable a man to live as a responsible person in the sight of God."**

We become responsible persons when we see ourselves as God sees us, or other people as God sees them, in emulation of the Christ who sees all yet does not turn away in disgust but in the midst of pain prays for his tormentors. "Father forgive them, for they know not what they do."

Long before then he had said, "Blessed are the peacemakers for they shall be called the children of God." Who does not desire peace or honor the peacemaker? On all sides we are beset by calls for strong, bold action for peace and warned of the deadly peril facing the human race if we do not achieve it. But action for peace will be productive only as we realize that men are both children of God—creatures of immense capacities—*and* sinners in need of pardon, and that we require pardon as much for our virtues as for our faults. Peace is not the absence of conflict, nor an escape from pain or trouble, nor even the earned consequence of a good conscience. Rather, peace is made by the forgiveness of God who accepts our efforts toward the good and continues to love us despite our failures, not least the failures that result from our blind, ignorant, and partial attempts to do the right. The peacemakers are those who know and acknowledge their own need for forgiveness, who come to realize that it was for them Jesus prayed when he said, "Father forgive them, for they know not what they do."

In Alan Paton's great novel *Too Late the Phalarope,* a police captain says, "There is a hard law . . . that when a deep injury is done to us we never recover until we forgive."*** It also is true that when we have inflicted deep injury we never really recover until we forgive ourselves, and we never completely forgive ourselves save as we know ourselves loved and forgiven,

---

* Dietrich Bonhoeffer, *Prisoner for God* (New York: The Macmillan Company, 1953), p. 18.

** *Ibid.,* p. 19.

*** Alan Paton, *Too Late the Phalarope* (New York: Charles Scribner's Sons, 1953), p. 266.

until the prayer of Christ to his Father is fulfilled in us and through us fulfilled in others.

Both this Beatitude and the prayer of Christ on the cross are gathered up by the author of the Epistle to the Ephesians who writes of Jesus, "He is our peace who has made us both one and has broken down the dividing wall of hostility . . . that he might create in himself one new man in place of the two, so making peace, and might reconcile us to God in one body through the cross thereby bringing the hostility to an end." (Ephesians 2:14–16 R.S.V.)

These words have a far wider application than the Jewish-Gentile tensions to which they were addressed in the first century. Our efforts toward peace need not be frantic, guilt-ridden attempts to earn a good conscience, but rather boundless struggles based on a forgiven and grateful conscience, looking to the Christ who is our peace and has broken down the dividing walls of hostility.

# III

# THE QUALITY OF MERCY

St. Luke 23:43     *"And he said to him, 'Truly I say to you, today you will be with me in paradise.'"* *(R.S.V.)*

St. Matthew 5:7     *"Blessed are the merciful, for they shall obtain mercy."* *(R.S.V.)*

THERE IS a wholeness about the Beatitudes that makes them seem more like a poem upon a certain quality of living than a category of separate virtues, for the qualities they describe so closely resemble each other that it is hard to separate them. For example, the peacemakers and the merciful are the same kinds of people. All the words from the cross, too, were spoken by the same man at the same time and some of them are much alike. We have written of forgiveness and how in receiving it and giving it we become the peacemakers who are the imitators and therefore the children of God. The second saying from the cross suggests the conditions under which forgiveness and mercy can be offered and received.

The crowd around the cross, cruel as crowds always are to a man who is down and defeated, was deriding Jesus with shouts such as "He saved others; he cannot save himself" (Matthew 27:42 R.S.V.), and, "Let the Christ, the King of Israel, come down from the cross that we may see and believe" (Matthew 27:42b), as if saving oneself and coming down from the cross would be signs of authenticity. To the taunts of the bystanders there now was added the mocking of one of the thieves, "Are not you the Messiah? Save yourself, and us" (Luke 23:39,40 N.E.B.).

In marked contrast was the response of the other: "Have you no fear of God? You are under the same sentence as he. For us it is plain justice; we are paying the price for our misdeeds; but this man has done nothing wrong." Then he said, "Jesus, remember me when you come to your throne."

Jesus answered, "I tell you this: today you will be with me in paradise." (Luke 23:40b–43 N.E.B.)

The contrasting responses of the thieves show the circumstances under which it is possible to give and obtain mercy as well as those under which such a gift is utterly impossible. Jesus could not show effective mercy to the first criminal. It was not that he did not want to; he surely must have loved and pitied him as much as he did the other. But he could not show mercy because this man really did not want it or, if he did, he narrowly interpreted mercy as being delivered from the consequences of his actions, his faults, and his follies.

Pardon cannot mean erasing all the consequences of foolish and evil deeds, or well-intentioned mistakes. Even God cannot do that in a universe in which he has permitted a measure of freedom to his creatures. It is folly, therefore, to approach Christ with a condition. "If I'm going to accept you, you must save me any pain for what I have done or failed to do; not only must you heal my wounds, you must also erase the scars."

Sometimes people approach the Church with such an attitude. The Church fails grossly and often, made up as it is of the imperfect, weak, sinful people such as ourselves. We who comprise the Church are called to serve the world and all the people in it, but we have neither the wisdom nor the power to cure all the world's ills, to turn evil into good everywhere on earth. This was well expressed by a penetrating English writer, Dr. D. R. Davies: "The cheek of modern man is colossal. He thinks he is doing the Church a good turn by graciously asking it to clean up his own mess." *

There are those who object to the entire concept of punishment, who maintain that we should protect society and rehabilitate the offender rather than punish him. Indeed there is much truth in this position. Harsh, extreme punishments are almost always a mistake, and all punishment should be remedial in intent, and wherever possible, in result. No one today would agree with the penitent thief that he and his companion were paying a just price for their misdeeds, that the torture of crucifixion is an appropriate penalty for theft. We like to think that we have made much progress in

* D. R. Davies, *The Two Humanities* (New York: Harper & Row, 1940), p. 225.

the treatment of crime since those rough and cruel days, yet as Dr. Karl Menninger points out in his recent book *The Crime of Punishment*,* we have regressed in some ways, such as keeping men behind bars for long periods of time, isolated, forgotten, bitter, and untreated.

Dr. Menninger's title is indeed apt, but if you dispense entirely with the concepts of punishment and penalty, do you not endanger human dignity and freedom? If no one is ever to be found guilty, who is innocent and who is free? No one may ever be entirely innocent before God, but everyone has a right to be presumed innocent by human society until proved guilty. If you do not stigmatize some kinds of conduct as unlawful, do you not end up by having to control all conduct for the public safety and for an alleged common good? Distinctions between good and evil cannot be erased without disaster even though specific ideas of what is right and what is wrong are not absolute but vary from culture to culture and from age to age as men become more sensitive or more callous, more wise or more foolish, more kind or more cruel, or as the environment under which they live changes. Love is the only absolute law of life, but the opposites of love are hate and indifference. Those who will not receive or give love are fated to receive wrath and live in coldness and isolation. Disaster overtakes those who love foolishly or irresponsibly. As a man sows he shall reap.

It is particularly urgent that those who belong to the privileged white middle and upper classes realize this, for it will help us to understand the anger, the irritation, and the dangerous confrontations and disruptions or the apathy of the poor, the black, and the young. We are living in a time of the reaping of the results of what has been sown for hundreds of years. This is not to deny how much has been accomplished in this land where people of all sorts from all over the world have been assimilated and where on the whole we have been developing an increasingly just and equitable society. These accomplishments underline the fact that we have only begun to deal with the consequences of bringing some of our oldest immigrants here forcibly and of keeping them and their children in slavery and subjection. This may be the time that God wills to remove this offense and, as Abraham Lincoln realized about slavery a hundred years ago, the offense cannot be removed painlessly or easily. Here is one of the crucial causes of the urban crisis.

In talking with black leaders I have been both impressed and depressed

---

*Karl Menninger, *The Crime of Punishment* (New York: The Viking Press, Inc., 1968).

by what many of them have said about violence. Few of them condoned it and even those who talked in violent terms seemed to be employing prophetic rhetoric rather than blatant threats. They knew that the backlash of violence was harmful to their people, were doing their best to prevent it, and yet seemed to have a sense of despair about avoiding it altogether, as if the suppressed anger of centuries could not help venting itself even though such action did no good to anyone, black or white.

No complacent satisfaction or fear on the part of the middle majority must deter us from moving strongly and fast. To bind up this nation's wounds, we must do our utmost to keep civil peace and order, all the while knowing that order without justice is tyranny. At the same time we must not be too surprised or impatient with uprisings or too harsh or ruthless in dealing with them. To expect to avoid them altogether may be as foolish and futile as were the words of the unrepentant thief, "Are you not the Messiah? Save yourself and us."

Nor is the anger and restlessness of the young surprising, belonging as they do to a generation that is coming to maturity at a time of great affluence and unrelieved poverty, unmanageable little wars in far-off places, and the threat of total annihilation. The shrewder of them have measured the gap between the profession and the performance of their elders, and have observed the unwillingness of the nation to tax itself to reclaim its cities, purify its air, rivers, and seas, and conserve its resources. The wiser of our children resentfully look forward to reaping the fruit of what others have sown, and to expect them to be quiet and acquiescent may be as feckless and unrealistic as was the cry of the unrepentant thief on the cross.

But the penitent thief could obtain mercy, for he asked for no escape from his sentence, simply that he be remembered with mercy as it was being inflicted and after it was over. To such a man Jesus could say, "Today you will be with me in paradise." (Luke 23:43 R.S.V.)

People often sneer at eleventh-hour repentance—what used to be called deathbed conversions, at least in the days before deathbeds were soothed with opiates. Obviously last-minute conversions need to be viewed with judgment, sometimes with skepticism, whether they take the form of reconciliation with a friend or a spouse or a new attitude toward race relations. But they do happen, and the test is not the hour in which they occur but their genuineness, their depth, and their result. Are we repenting in order to be taken down from the cross? Do we care more about God's will than about being right, more about responsible action for good in the world than about our reputations, our principles, or even our characters? Do we seek to eliminate injustice and poverty only because we feel that the effect of them will boomerang on us?

Most people do act from self-interest. It is very hard to further a good cause in a community unless the people can be convinced that the cause is in their own interest. Even the highest dedication to good causes is usually tinged with self-interest. But there may be moments when we forget this, when we turn to Christ, share his agony over the sufferings of the least of his brothers, and ask only that he will give us a part in the establishment of his kingdom.

"Today you will be with me in paradise." Like the other Beatitudes the one about the merciful obtaining mercy has a future promise with it, a promise of joy and peace when the purpose of God is fulfilled, and when his kingdom comes. It contains the assurance that the significance of our personal lives is not limited to this world or to the particular time in which we live, but that God will use us and what we do forever. This use of us begins now, today.

In the time of Christ the word "paradise" had a nebulous, shadowy meaning, somehow associated with the realm of the departed spirits. To say that "today you will be with me in paradise" meant "beginning today you and I will share the future, share eternity together." In this assurance paradise comes to earth. What happens beyond this earth we do not know, yet where Jesus went no man need fear to go. Already he has descended to the realm of the departed spirits and turned that place into paradise.

Jesus was merciful, not in overlooking evil but in accepting evil men, identifying with them to the point of death and beyond death.

This was expressed by the 14th-century German artist Grünewald in a picture he painted to hang in a hospital for syphilitics. The picture shows Christ on the cross with the sores and ravages of syphilis on his body. No one imagined that Jesus himself had syphilis, but those who did could look at the picture and know that they were embraced by his mercy.

This was the man who said, "Blessed are the merciful for they shall obtain mercy." (Matthew 5:7.) Blessed are those who do not gloat over the punishments that others bring upon themselves. Blessed are those so sure of God's mercy that they feel no need to rejoice in other people's misfortunes, no need to be glad to see others go wrong, no need to resent hearing of the gifts and the virtues of others, no need to seek revenge, no need to be inhibited from rejoicing in others' successes.

This conversation of Christ with the thieves helps save us from impatiently demanding that we be taken down from crosses of our own making. It can save us from the need of proving ourselves right or even thinking ourselves right and free us to repent and make amends when we are wrong. It can save us from a self-righteous debauch and the misery of further separation from the mercy of God. It can help us forgive ourselves and live with the irrevocable consequences of our mistakes. It can save us from punishing without restoring. It assures us of the companionship of Christ upon the crosses that are inevitable and irremoveable.

In his novel *Crime and Punishment* Dostoevski shows how punishment leads to renewal for Raskolnikov and Sonia. "They wanted to speak, but could not; tears stood in their eyes. They were both pale and thin; but those sick, pale faces were bright with the dawn of a new future, of a full resurrection into a new life. They were renewed by love; the heart of each held infinite sources of life for the heart of the other."*

---

\* Fedor Dostoevski, *Crime and Punishment* (New York: Random House, Inc., 1956), p. 331.

# IV

# THE HUMBLE MADE GREAT

St. John 19:26–27   *"When Jesus saw his mother, and the disciple whom he loved standing near, he said to his mother, 'Woman, behold, your son!' Then he said to the disciple, 'Behold, your mother!' And from that hour the disciple took her to his own home." (R.S.V.)*

St. Matthew 5:5   *"Blessed are the meek, for they shall inherit the earth." (R.S.V.)*

Among the public assassinations of the 1960's the death of Martin Luther King had a particularly poignant character, perhaps because he represented and embodied the hope that the oppressed could secure justice without violence. He was buried in a ceremony of simple grandeur with the nation's great in attendance and much of the country's business halted while millions paid tribute. Eric Sevareid characterized that day, that fell appropriately in Holy Week, as one when the great had been made humble and the humble made great. If he was right it was a day of fulfillment of the words of Jesus, "Blessed are the meek, for they shall inherit the earth." In symbol at least the meek did inherit the earth for those few hours.

Rarely do the meek inherit the earth in so vivid and dramatic a manner. Usually they are pushed aside, used, taken advantage of and exploited, unnoticed in life and forgotten in death.

The mother of Jesus was that way, at least during the time she lived on earth. For all the honor and exaltation that has been given to her in the Christian Church she is one of history's best examples of her son's saying, "Blessed are the meek, for they shall inherit the earth."

Throughout almost the whole of the Gospel story she is in the background, seldom speaking at all. We have very little idea of what she was like, what she thought, or how she lived. In the story of the Annunciation when the Angel Gabriel tells her she is to be the mother of Christ she replies, "Behold, I am the handmaid of the Lord, let it be to me according to your word." (Luke 1:38 R.S.V.) The remainder of her life was a continual following of this original obedience.

When her son was presented in the temple as a baby, the aged Simeon prophetically warned her, "A sword will pierce through your own soul." (Luke 2:35 R.S.V.) That sword never left her unscathed for very long.

Most parents have had the annoying and fearful experience of losing track of their children in the neighborhood or on a trip; few parents have lost their children for three days and found them in church, as Mary did when her son was twelve years old, and received the confusing and what might have seemed unctuous answer, "Did you not know that I must be in my Father's house?" (Luke 2:49 R.S.V.)

She never seems to have understood the strange, unconventional career of her son in any fullness. How embarrassing to her must have been the scene in the home synagogue in Nazareth when he preached such a tactless sermon and was thrown out and almost lynched before her eyes. Mothers like to feel proud of their children when they come home and appear in public after acquiring a reputation elsewhere.

Then there was the time when relatives and townspeople began to hint that he was beside himself, so strangely was he behaving, and she took his brothers with her to Capernaum to bring him home. When she arrived at the house where he was teaching and sent a message in to him through the crowd that they wished to see him, he only replied "Who are my mother and my brothers?" Then he looked around at those who sat about him and said, "Here are my mothers and my brothers. Whoever does the will of God is my brother and sister and mother." (Matthew 12:48,50 R.S.V.) What mother would not be cut by such a rebuke, yet she had no choice but to accept the fact that he belonged to a larger family.

On Good Friday she stood on Calvary looking upon all the humiliation and shame of the cross, watching her son suffer and unable to do anything to relieve his agony. When this became too much for her to bear, he commended her to the care of the beloved disciple. Again she was sent away into the background.

Blessed are the meek. Blessed are those who live in the shadows of the mighty, who must pick up for the mighty and cover for the famous, bearing

their children, raising their families, making homes for those so absorbed in
the business and the struggles of a larger world that they often ignore
ruthlessly those closest to them. It has been said that it takes a saint to live
with a saint. Brave and blessed is the widow of the hero who so shares his
purpose that she carries on his work for years afterward, as does Coretta
King.

It is not easy to take second place and yet most of us must do that. It is
not easy to have your children grow away from you in thought and in
interest or even in affection, at least as far as their primary attachment goes.
Yet all parents must face that. Only foolish and insecure parents try to
prevent it. Wise parents accept it gracefully, and often come to rejoice in it.

It is not easy to retire, and it is particularly hard to leave a position of
influence and affluence, where people have deferred to you and looked to
you for leadership, even done you the compliment of opposing you and
criticizing your ideas. A former President of the United States complained
that people kept bothering him with requests for favors and opinions and
of the crowds who drove down the street where he lived, stood gawking
at his home, taking photographs of it and hoping that he would appear. A
friend listened to this man's complaints and made the shrewd reply, "How
much worse you will feel when they start ignoring you." Those who have
served in high echelons of government will recall ruefully the power that is
is gone, the splendid cars and chauffeurs, the publicity, the public attention
and the private protection which they once enjoyed. Some are bitter, some
aimlessly lost, but among them are the truly meek who find fulfillment in
new ways of living and serving.

Then there are the great numbers of people all over the world, largely
unknown even to each other, who strive to make the human condition
more just, more compassionate, more joyful; who by acts of consideration
and kindness constantly enrich the quality of the common life. Many of them
belong to the Church of Christ but their number spreads beyond the visible
membership of the Church. Indeed, it includes all who serve the brothers
of Christ and in doing so serve Christ himself, just as truly as did the
soldier who held the sponge full of vinegar to his parched lips. Each one of us
remembers people of this sort in our neighborhoods, in our parishes, as
fellow workers in the many volunteer agencies that do so much to keep
the life of the nation more fair, more just, and more healthful. I think of
those I met in Vietnam three years ago repairing the ravages and wounds
of war. Some were Vietnamese civilians, others American military personnel,

civilian workers, members of the historic peace churches who refuse to bear arms, but do not shrink from labor involving much hardship and danger. I think of the church societies and the clergy, the priests and the nuns who were relieving suffering, sheltering families, feeding children under conditions of incredible difficulty. When the story of Vietnam is written, these folk will be remembered as well as will the massacres, the destruction, the pain and death, and the questionable foreign policy that produced them all.

Then I recall a trip to East Africa to visit a group of Christians with whom the diocese of which I was then the bishop had a special companion link. There I met men and women who spoke in very simple terms of how they had been found and saved by Jesus Christ. I remember their humble eagerness to impart their saving knowledge to others and of thinking how much they might give to us had we the meekness to listen and to receive from them.

Among the meek are many of those who are separated from us by the political and national divisions that men make and exaggerate into iron curtains, into almost impassable barriers. But no such barrier is completely impassable when people are humble enough, curious enough, and open enough to listen to each other. There are the Christian-Marxist dialogues taking place in small groups, with Christians and Communists learning from each other, discovering what is true in a position toward which they have been accustomed to be hostile, even submitting to mutual correction at each other's hands. There are the Christians in places such as Hanoi or China. Many of them are comparatively new Christians. Like us they feel called upon to be loyal to their own country, to help build their own society without betraying their loyalty to Christ. We hear little from them but much of what we hear indicates that they are carrying on with both courage and subtlety.

The twentieth century has often been called a time of greatness. It is a time for greatness, but it is also a time for meekness because the issues of this age are too great for any one person to comprehend, much less to solve. Under such circumstances pressures of all sorts bear heavily upon almost everyone. There is the pressure of population, with the poor of the underdeveloped nations already hungry and facing future famine and starvation. There are the affluent nations wasting their resources and polluting their riches, with pockets of poverty and with their poor increasingly bitter and resentful. There is the so-called Establishment, bewildered by the complexities of governing nations, planning economies, managing industries, and providing the resources of education, health, and welfare. There is the new Middle

America, containing many angry, fearful people, feeling pushed between the poor and the Establishment, complaining that no one listens to them, dismayed by what they believe to be threats to the standards and values by which they have lived and achieved no small measure of success. In our confused current condition, among our best hopes are the meek who refuse to be stampeded by lies, fear, and slander, who face each day as it comes, gallantly and courageously, and then, like Mary, trust God for the result even though God's ways seem strange and the world's ways perverse.

Many of us feel guilty that we are not doing more. Others are overwhelmed even to the point of apathy, have ceased to hope, and are "opting out." We must do what we can, and there are times when we can do little more than think and talk, vote and act, as honestly and wisely as possible. Our vocation may be no more nor less important than that of a certain innkeeper on the road from Jerusalem to Jericho without whom the Good Samaritan never could have found a place to bring the man who had been beaten by thieves and left lying on the road. Or we may be among those who keep the traffic moving while buildings are being constructed along the highway, or when a new subway line is being created under a busy street.

It was Mary herself, recalling an Old Testament hymn, who sang words much like those of Eric Sevareid. "For behold, henceforth all generations will call me blessed; for he who is mighty has done great things for me . . . he has put down the mighty from their thrones, and exalted those of low degree." (Luke 1:48b–52 R.S.V.) She was a witness to the Resurrection; she lost her son in death but she found him as risen Saviour and Lord. Many times in Christian history she has been the center of intimate devotion and sentiment and continues to be so over much of the Christian world today. Some may question this, but it is surely understandable, for there are multitudes whose experience so closely resembles that of this woman that her companionship is precious beyond words.

Jesus shared his mother's meekness, not, to be sure, in the soft, mild manner we sometimes associate with that quality. He was strong and he was forceful but he was also meek. He spoke and acted with authority but it was a meek authority, in some ways an offensive authority. He confronted men with their condition, he rudely upset their complacency, but he did not force them to follow him nor make them dependent upon him nor solve their problems for them. There were times when crowds flocked to him, but on the whole he was not a man who went in for big public demonstrations. Even the triumphal entry on Palm Sunday was more like a commotion in the inner city, resembling a parade in Harlem more than a cavalcade up Fifth Avenue with tickertape and confetti thrown from the windows. The cleansing of the temple was more like a sit-in, and a brief one at that, than a take-over of power. John the Baptist was almost surely a better known figure in first-century Palestine than was Jesus of Nazareth. John's name appears in nonbiblical literature while the name of Jesus does not, and the movement started by John the Baptist persisted alongside that of the Christian Church for several decades.

As we think of the meekness of Mary and the meekness of Christ we think also of the meekness of God. God, too, stays in the background; he hides himself, he refuses to force his love upon us, he does not solve our problems for us. As Dietrich Bonhoeffer put it, he expects us to act as men come-of-age rather than as dependent children; he is not to be found in sacred places nor to be manipulated by holy practices. He is at the center of life, yet allows himself to be edged out of the world onto the cross. He is most in character not when he is creating the universe with its vast interstellar space, its planets and its galaxies; he is most God not when he is wielding the power in the atom, but when in meekness and in love he suffers at the hands of the men he has made.

And here is his ultimate power; here is the meekness that inherits the earth in resurrection and victory. That is why we believe that Eric Sevareid's characterization of one particular day as the time when the great had been made humble and the humble made great was not merely a statement of the significance of that one occasion but an affirmation of sure hope for the long future.

# V

## WHILE WE MOURN
## THERE IS HOPE

St. Mark 15:34    *"And at the ninth hour Jesus cried with a loud voice, 'Eloi, Eloi, lama sabachthani,' which means, 'My God, my God, why hast thou forsaken me?'" (R.S.V.)*

St. Matthew 5:4    *"Blessed are those who mourn, for they shall be comforted." (R.S.V.)*

THERE WAS a darkness over the whole land the day Christ died. There has been darkness over our whole land during much of the past decade. There was darkness in Dallas one bright November day; there was darkness during one April week despite an early and lovely spring. There is darkness in Vietnam although few countries in the world are more beautiful when one views its wide beaches and lush mountains from the air. There has been much darkness over the whole world during recent generations with total war, saturation bombing, and death camps; and this despite all the advances in creature-comforts, in affluence, and in the conquest of disease and death.

This twentieth-century darkness has in no small measure been responsible for what has been called the Death-of-God theology. That particular theology seems to have come and gone, but many of the questions it raised are still with us. How can there be a living God who cares when one considers the new dimensions of tragedy in our time? A rabbi told a group of students not long ago that one could not believe in the traditional God of the Jews and the Christians without considering him "a first-grade s.o.b." "My God, my God, why has thou forsaken me?"

But this is no new darkness. It was well known to the Hebrew people long before the time of Christ and it invaded his soul as he was dying alone, rejected by his people, ridiculed by his enemies, deserted by his friends. The departure of his mother and the beloved disciple must have intensified his loneliness and isolation. It is always hard to say farewell to those whom you love, particularly if you know it is the last farewell. In this case it was farewell forever, for no matter how strongly we believe in eternal life, death does end this mortal life with its relationships and satisfactions. Anything beyond must be very different indeed.

Did Jesus wonder whether or not his Father in heaven cared about him? Did he ask whether the vision at his baptism when the heavens opened and the voice told him "Thou art my beloved son" had not been an empty dream? Many thrilling dreams have a way of disappearing in the cold reality of the day, and this was a very terrible day. Could the Devil have been right in slyly suggesting in the wilderness, "If you are the Son of God . . . ," with great stress on the "if"? Indeed, Satan has a way of undermining us with that word "if."

Turning to the ancient psalms for comfort, his words rose to a cry as he recited the opening verse of the twenty-second Psalm, "My God, my God, why hast thou forsaken me?"

Long before this he had said, "Blessed are those who mourn, for they shall be comforted." Blessed are those who in times of despondency, temptation, and despair can call to mind words of men who have shared similar dark experiences, especially the words of men that have comforted many generations and centuries of people. Undoubtedly our Lord knew many of the psalms by heart and therefore realized he was not alone in his sense of abandonment and despair, for you will find such emotions expressed over and over again throughout the entire Psalter and in many of the prophets. Those who are familiar with the expressions of our faith as they are found in the Bible, or Prayer Book, or hymnals, or in many of the devotional classics, are fortunate indeed, for those books and those words lead us to the discovery that many men and women throughout history have traveled the same road that we walk today. Some opiates used after major surgery do not deaden the pain as much as they take away the memory of it and therefore make it more transitory and bearable. The classic statements of our faith may not make our loneliness or frustration any less acute but they make it more endurable by relating it to the long memory of the human race.

To read history is to know that there is no new dimension of tragedy in the twentieth century; no, not after the cruelty of the Assyrian Empire or the destruction of Jerusalem and any number of cities many times, or Ghengis

Khan, or the Children's Crusade, or the Massacre of St. Bartholomew's Day, or the Inquisition. The history of mankind has been a history of blood and tears. The dimensions of tragedy may seem larger today because there are more people to suffer or because tragedy is more widely reported or because almost every new scientific advance is somehow perverted to demonic use, but the essential dimensions retain their grim sameness.

Jesus, then, knew the despair and isolation that come when all our efforts seem to have failed, when our motives are misjudged, when no one appreciates or responds to our attempts to help or our efforts to serve and when even the support of heaven seems completely withdrawn.

There are many people for whom the disasters, the horrors, and the pain of life make faith in God's goodness impossible to hold; there seems to be no purpose, no reason, no meaning, and no value in such suffering. This is what has made compassionate men talk about the death of God.

But this very doubt can be a sign of a searching faith, a faith not content with easy answers, an honest faith, not satisfied until it has taken account of all the frightful facts that men must face. G. K. Chesterton once wrote some lines praying to be delivered "from all the easy speeches that comfort cruel men," and Dietrich Bonhoeffer wrote from prison during a series of heavy Allied air raids on Berlin, "I am afraid however I make a bad comforter; I can listen all right, but hardly ever find anything to say. But perhaps the way one asks about some things and is silent about others helps to suggest what really matters. . . . It does seem to me more important that we should really experience certain kinds of distress rather than try to bottle it up or explain it away.*

It has been truly said that Christianity creates the problem of pain before it presumes to meet it. Pain would be just a fact and not a theological problem at all unless the Christian Gospel asserted the goodness of God. So our very rebellion against suffering and our questioning of a God who permits pain can themselves be a sign of a faith that transcends suffering as well as of a sensitivity and openness to the suffering of others. Thus the cynic and the agnostic can be more compassionate than the idealist or the superficial believer. Few men have been more affected by the world's pain than Bertrand Russell, the allegedly free unbeliever.

The despair of Jesus was a result of mourning over the suffering of others as well as his own. As long as we mourn, as long as we care, God will guide

* *Prisoner for God, Ibid.*, pp. 98, 99.

us into the active pity that releases us from despair. We are unlikely to remain depressed when we are absorbed in serving others.

There is all the difference in the world between being so sensitive that we mourn and in being so hard that we become bitter. Often we are tempted to become hard in order to remain sane. But those who have become hardened in bitterness have entered an emotional blind alley protecting themselves rather than reaching out to others. As long as you can weep there is hope. Pitiable are those who can no longer weep.

The cry, "Why hast thou forsaken me?" plumbs the depths of Christ's suffering; it must also reveal the depth of his Father's suffering. What could have more pierced the heart of God than to know that his son felt forsaken by him? Parents feel devastated when their small children have been badly hurt and cry to these parents in uncomprehending pain. The same parents feel even more desolate when their older children face the anxiety, the doubts, and the conflicts of growing up. We grieve when we see our friends make what we regard as stupid and disastrous mistakes that we are powerless to prevent. But God stood by and watched his son die in such agony that for a short time at least he felt forsaken by his Father. What other assurance need we that God grieves over our present sufferings and will turn the pain of his people to good account? "Blessed are those who mourn, for they shall be comforted."

Jesus was comforted. Perhaps this began as he remembered through to the end of the twenty-second Psalm. "Men shall tell of the Lord to the coming generations and proclaim his deliverance to a people yet unborn." We shall overcome.

The contrast between the beauty of this created world, the events of recent years and the people involved in them, and the cross itself has been expressed in a poem written on the day that Martin Luther King was buried, but speaking to much more than that single event.

> There is a bird that sings
> and there are flowers.
>
> I have wept
> the tears of sorrow down my cheeks
>
> standin' there
> standin' there
> water come to me eye

come back
come back
wipe the tears from me eye!

They do not want to let him go.
They sing.
They pray
and sing again. They
do not want to let him go.

House built on a weak foundation
will not stand o no

"I have a dream . . .

I have a dream . . . !"

hosanna build a house o

"I do not know—I do not know—
I do not know
How long . . . but

I have a dream."

The way was long to go.
The sun was hot.

He lead the way and
we walked

The way is long.

Nailed on a black cross
and spat upon
and reviled

water come to me eye

standin' there
standin' there

I'm tired. I'm tired. Take my hand. Take my hand.

Not as I am. Not as I am—alone,
but with you

not alone—not white—not slave—not free
we pray
and we sing

to pray together!
to sing together!

Hold my hand.

We shall overcome.

I do not know—I do not know—
how long?

House built on a strong foundation
it will stand o yes

The grass lies trampled.
The sky light dims.
I'm home.

There are flowers and
there is a bird that sings.

There's love.


"Blessed are those who mourn, for they shall be comforted."

# VI

# THE ULTIMATE HUNGER

St. John 19:28   *"After this Jesus, knowing that all was now finished, said (to fulfill the scripture), 'I thirst.'" (R.S.V.)*

St. Matthew 5:6   *"Blessed are those who hunger and thirst for righteousness, for they shall be satisfied." (R.S.V.)*

I THIRST" appears to be merely a simple request for a drink made by a man in great pain. It is hardly a surprising plea, for one of the severest tortures of crucifixion was the dehydration of the body, increasing the agony of anyone who lingered on a cross for any length of time. On the surface, then, this statement calls for little comment, but there are meanings and nuances in our seemingly most simple words, especially when spoken at critical moments of our lives. Furthermore the Church has always been inclined to go below the surface in interpreting the words of scripture, especially the words of Christ.

The words "I thirst" underscore the fact that our Lord was completely and fully human. Like all men he needed to eat and drink. Unlike many committed and devout men such as John the Baptist, Jesus apparently enjoyed eating and drinking. His enemies accused him of being a glutton and a drunkard. Many of the stories about him have as their setting meals eaten with his disciples and his friends and the conversations that went with them. There are also stories of quarrels with his critics at meals, of his shrewd observation of their social ambitions and their eagerness to be respectable.

He realized man's need for bread and he fed hungry crowds with bread and fish. But in the desert he reminded Satan that man does not live by bread alone; he used bread and wine to convey himself, the bread of life. Now on the cross his strength ebbs more quickly than the strength of those who are dying with him. He who has fed the multitudes and healed the sick must ask his executioners for a drink of water.

This word from the cross and the stories and teaching of Jesus centering about eating and drinking suggest consideration of the things that people desire. Hunger and thirst do typify our wants. Everyone must eat and drink; God made us that way and likes us that way. It is foolish, even hypocritical, for the Church to set itself up as more spiritual than God and for well-fed Christians to ignore the hunger of the poor while talking to them of their alleged spiritual needs.

Everyone must eat and drink, but there are many other things tangible and less tangible that people embrace with the eagerness that they have for food and water. Thus the words hunger and thirst are used to connote man's craving for sex, for love, for companionship, for almost anything that human beings want.

While Jesus thirsted on the cross, that cross was surrounded by a world of desires different from that thirst, yet related to it. And because in a very real sense the cross is a permanent part of the human scene and because Jesus continues in agony until the end of the world the cross is still surrounded by a world of human desires, varied, often uncoordinated, and frequently chaotic. This has been expressed in an unpublished poem "Way of the Cross":

> The cross is outlined against
> the darkening sky—
>
> a child shrieks and laughs,
> running through an alley
> in a game of play—
>
> His body is racked with pain
> and torture is—
>
> the couple cling closely in
> hot embraces and drown
> themselves in love—

His voice is barely above a
whisper and, "I thirst"—

the market place is crowded
and she touches fruit
with loving hands—

His eyes are closed, and blood
is dripping—

the old man flails a cane,
and anger rises in waves
against his son—

The cross is outlined against
the darkened sky,
and suffering
is born.

For Jesus desire was not uncoordinated and chaotic. He said, "Blessed are those who hunger and thirst for righteousness, for they shall be filled." He had committed himself to one absorbing pursuit, following God's will for his life. "My food is to do the will of him who sent me and to accomplish his work." (John 4:34 R.S.V.) His hunger was to be about his Father's business; he compared the kingdom of heaven to hidden treasure which a man finds in a field and then sells all that he has to buy that field, or to a pearl of great price discovered by a merchant who then sells all that he has to buy it.

Happy is a man with such an aim. Most of us are torn between a host of conflicting desires. We try to satisfy many of them but rarely pursue any one of them to the full. There are gaps between our intentions and our performances resembling the detours on the highways along which we travel.

Of course, we all believe in righteousness. Who does not? Almost everyone is sincere and wants to do the right things. Most of the harm we do is done with good intention. But our righteousness is rarely the sort for which anyone would hunger but more like the product of a cheap restaurant with cracked dishes, tarnished silverware, and poorly cooked and sloppily served food. People eat in cheap restaurants because they cannot afford better ones and the cheapness of our contemporary righteousness reveals our lack of capacity to spend and be spent. We are the heirs of a great tradition but have done little to replenish or increase our inheritance.

Our idea of righteousness tends to approximate that of our community, of our friends and associates, of the world around us. You abstain from well-known vices, or at least you are very discreet when you indulge in them. You conform to the code of your set, you obey the law, at least the laws of which you and your friends approve or believe it unwise or destructive to violate. But you are still free to keep your hates, to enjoy your prejudices, to use people for your own ends with little concern for theirs, to indulge in gossip and slander that is not too savage, and never to examine the premises upon which you order your conduct.

But for Jesus righteousness was a consuming, driving obsession. When we speak of him as sinless we do not mean that all his opinions were neces-sarily correct, that he never made a mistake, that he did not become irritated nor lose his temper, that he was a grown-up little Lord Fauntleroy. Rather we mean that there was no significant unfilled gap between his own desire and what he saw as his Father's will for his life. He knew that the finest things in anyone's life could not be had for the wishing or the asking and for them he was prepared to pay the price of the cross.

Nor was the righteousness for which he hungered and thirsted a narrow, legalistic, world-denying righteousness. He talked of perfection and by that he meant integrity of one's whole life, and yet he was a friend of collaborationist tax collectors and disreputable outcasts. He was not interested in manicuring minor moralities but commanded a love that reached out even to his enemies. He demanded discipline, not for its own sake but in service for the kingdom. He sat lightly on rules about the Sabbath, diet, an ceremonial cleanliness. This was a dangerous thing to do for it was those very rules that helped identify the Jews as the people of God. But Jesus knew that he lived in a time when the coming of the kingdom required the re-evaluation of old rules and the scrapping of some of them. Saint Paul truly interpreted Christ when he wrote of love as the fulfilling of the law. To hunger and thirst for righteousness is to seek a righteousness of freedom, truth, imagination, and adventure.

If contemporary events have taught us anything at all, they have shown us that we are in sore need of such righteousness. As a nation we are a people of good intentions. Perhaps no people in all history have had better intentions and certainly no people in history have been more eager to have their good intentions recognized, more anxious to be thought right, than have modern Americans. Indeed, that is a great part of our problem, for no people who have acquired wealth and power can use their power and resources with rectitude all the time. Good intentions by themselves are sterile unless accompanied with a hunger and thirst for the righteousness of a just God calling us to put an end to the unnecessary injustices of our society and to replace slavery to our conventional and self-righteous opinions by free obedience to God in love of all his creatures.

This is the sort of righteousness that many of the finest of our young people of our time are seeking. We may think them extreme or intolerant or unconventional or as sitting lightly on traditional moral codes. Underneath all this is frequently found a passion for righteousness, an anger at injustice, a demand for honesty, a willingness to alter standards to conform to new facts and new truths, a passion to combat evil and relieve suffering that cannot be far from the kingdom of God.

Hunger and thirst for such righteousness are nowhere more needed than in the Church today, where there are signs that the righteousness of the Church has fallen below that of certain other segments of our society. Is it not a judgment on our alleged righteousness that the Supreme Court of the United States and the armed forces of the United States have been more effective in lessening racial segregation in our country than the churches that bear the name of Jesus Christ? We may deplore the slow pace of the integration of our public schools but these schools are far less segregated than our Christian congregations. I do not overlook the role of creative minorities within the churches nor the courageous actions of many denominations in their official assemblies and at top levels of leadership. Immeasurably important contributions have been made, although fairly recent sociological studies show that, statistically speaking, one is more likely to be actively concerned about removing social injustice if he does not attend church than if he does. It is also fair to say that there has been a more forthright facing of what has been called the sexual revolution outside the Church than inside it, as we find that established codes and folkways regarding marriage and sexual behavior need to be re-evaluated at a time of overpopulation, safer contraception, greater longevity, and the uprooted mobility of people in an urban culture.

Jesus promised that those who hunger and thirst after righteousness would be filled with peace, with power, with joy. Many of life's hungers never can be satisfied. Other hungers are satisfied but even their satisfaction leaves one restless and disillusioned. The psalmist wrote, "He gave them their heart's desire and sent leanness withal into their souls." (Psalm 106:15 K.J.V.) To describe such leanness a cynic has written a new Beatitude: "Blessed is he who expects nothing, for he shall not be disappointed." There are far too many people who have been disappointed so many times that they trust no one and expect nothing. Such apathy eats away the hope and ambition of a great many people at the present time. It infects the spirit and the attitude of large numbers of the young, making them wonder, What's the use? What can we look forward to? Is there any point in trying? Here is one of the basic causes of what has been called the drug subculture.

Jesus did expect much. He asked for a drink and received it; he trusted in God and was not disappointed. Unless we can recover such trust we will be disillusioned and disappointed; unless we can recover a lost sense of transcendence all our maps and directions for this world will be distorted and deceptive; unless we hunger and thirst after God's righteousness we will find any attempt to establish our own frustrating and fruitless. For man is made to ask the ultimate questions.

Christ assures us, "Ask and it will be given you, seek and you will find; knock and it will be opened to you. . . . I am the bread of life, he who comes to me shall not hunger, and he who believes in me shall never thirst." (Matthew 7:7; John 6:35 R.S.V.)

We shall seek God who is our righteousness that in finding we may have to give.

# VII

## FREEDOM TO FINISH

---

St. John 19:30     *"When Jesus had received the vinegar, he said, 'It is finished' and he bowed his head and gave up his spirit." (R.S.V.)*

St. Matthew 5:3     *"Blessed are the poor in spirit: for theirs is the kingdom of heaven." (K.J.V.)*

---

WHEN IS one's work finished?

I am sure that many of us would answer, "Never," especially if we are people with business, professional, or public responsibilities, if we compose music or paint pictures, or if we have a home and family for which to care. We feel pressed and crowd all we can into every hour of the day and often into the night as well.

If we have been elected to a particular office for any length of time or if we know we must retire next year or in five years, we begin to be anxious about how much we can accomplish in the time we have left. The dying words of Pope Pius XI were said to have been, "Still so much to do."

This is called an age of leisure. While some people who are retired or who have repetitive sorts of jobs and enjoy a shortened work week may find themselves feeling empty and bored, with time on their hands which they do not know how to occupy, those in positions of leadership and many others besides never seem to catch up with all that there is to do. This may be an age of leisure. It is also an age of urgency in which informed, sensitive people have a feeling that the time is short for the human race. Between now and the beginning of the twenty-first century we either will have taken decisive steps to ensure peace, to avoid total destruction either by war or choking pollution of the environment, to check the unbridled growth of population, or we will have lost control of our destiny, with the prospect that man as a species will be farther along the road to extinction than he would have imagined a fairly short time ago. So we feel we must act and act quickly even though we are not sure of just what we should do. If we are asked to undertake work that seems essential for the good of the community, the nation, or the parish, we are apt to feel guilty if we do not agree to do it, even though we are already involved in more presumably worthwhile activities than we possibly can do well.

But Jesus said, "It is finished" in his early thirties, an age when many men think that most of life is before them and feel themselves to be embarking upon the most productive parts of their careers. In a few short years of public ministry, according to some authorities only a few months, he had made his mark for all time and had accomplished enough for all the centuries to build upon.

Yet this must seem more true in retrospect than it would have appeared at the time. If we had known him then, we might well have regarded his death as an unmitigated tragedy. If any man were ever indispensable, it could have seemed that Jesus Christ would be that person. This is particularly true if some recent scholars are correct in believing him to be involved closely with the radical Zealot movement aimed at the collaborationist priestly class in Jerusalem and at securing Israel's independence from Rome. Had he continued as a living political force, the movement might have been led in such a way that the disastrous revolt of the late sixties would have been avoided and Jerusalem saved from ravaging and destruction. Even if the more conventional view of Jesus' ministry is the true one, if he remained independent of the main political currents of the period and in a sense stood in judgment upon all of them, one could still regard his death as a disaster. In either case might it not have been wiser for him to have stayed in the background and allowed others to represent him publicly as they were accustomed to doing when he sent them out on missions to preach, teach, and heal? Could he not have gone underground for a while? Might it not have been the better part of wisdom and sounder strategy not to force an issue just at that time with a hostile chief priest in Jerusalem and with the Roman authority obviously anxious about public order in a volatile and explosive community, crowded with visitors, pilgrims, and plotters? Were not the staged entry into Jerusalem, the cleansing of the temple, and the bitter public debates within its precincts a rather reckless challenge for a man without the power to make it effective? Suppose he had retired to a quiet spot and bided his opportunity. He might have spent years teaching increasing numbers of people and perhaps had the joy of seeing them come to understand his messages. Or, if his ambitions were political, he might have trained followers for action at the right time and place. Then there were multitudes of sick, distressed, and disturbed people who needed him and whom he had not yet been able to reach; he might relieve the misery and heal the sickness of many of them. Certainly the instincts of the prophet and the pastor must have warred within him just as they do within the heart of any man who is both zealous and compassionate. Then there were the children who had flocked to him so eagerly. Children are said to be more teachable than adults; certainly they are more open and malleable. Might not these same children have grown in their understanding of his teaching had he been around longer? Might they not have become some of his strongest leaders? Jesus must have been greatly tempted both by his ambition and by his love of people. Perhaps such thoughts contributed to the intensity of his agony in the garden on the Mount of Olives on the night before he died. "Father, if it be possible, let this cup pass from me; nevertheless not as I will, but as thou wilt." (Matthew 26:39 R.S.V.)

There is the awful humility running through the discourses of Christ at the Last Supper as reported in Saint John's Gospel. These may not be the words of Jesus, but they are put into his mouth in a profoundly true understanding of the meaning of his ministry. "It is to your advantage that I go away, for if I do not go away the Counsel will not come to you; but if I go, I will send him to you . . . when the Spirit of Truth comes, he will guide you into all truth . . . he who believes in me will also do the work that I do; and greater works than these will you do because I go to the Father." (John 16:7,13; 14:12 R.S.V.)

Christ was under no illusions about himself. His greatest success was not in the days of his ministry in Palestine; instead, his most significant accomplishments came through the Holy Spirit after his resurrection and glorification. This is shown by the lives of the apostles; they were weak, dull, and inept during much of the time that Jesus was with them. They did not seem to improve with time, for their rivalry over position continued right up to the eve of Good Friday. They ran away in a crisis and one of them denied all relationship with him only a short time after boasting that he would be faithful whatever disaster might come; of course, Judas betrayed him for reasons that no one really understands to this day. It may be encouraging to teachers to remember that the greatest of all teachers was a flat failure with one out of twelve of the pupils he had most carefully chosen and to whom he gave the most time and attention and that his success with the other eleven was very mixed at best. But when these apostles had gone through the experiences of Easter and Pentecost, when they were commissioned anew by the risen Christ, they became unconquerable with only occasional traces of their former weakness and vacillation.

Here I think is the difference between Christ and many other folk heroes. Abraham Lincoln has become a legend, but as a man and a force his influence ceased soon after April 14, 1865. The memory of Ghandi is revered as a combination of a saint and a canny politician who knew just what kind of power to use to achieve Indian independence, but he is hardly a force men follow in India. The extent to which Martin Luther King's nonviolent struggles will mold the immediate future of America is hard to know; many militant black people thought that he was becoming irrelevant at the time of his death. Confucius is honored for his teaching rather than his person and Mohammed is revered as the prophet who founded a faith based upon an unchanging Koran. Buddha's teachings are cherished and his example multiplied by many holy people who are said to incarnate his spirit. But more people know Jesus Christ as a living reality today than ever knew him when he lived on earth. There is actually more evidence of the fact that he rose from the dead than that he lived at all in the first place and this is because of the way he lived and died, because he exemplified his own words, "Blessed are the poor in spirit for theirs is the kingdom of heaven."

This Beatitude identifies those who are not swayed by a sense of their immediate importance and who are willing to carry on the work that God gives them whether the job takes one year or a lifetime. But because it is God's work, not theirs—only God's work is perfect and no man's ever is—they can always say, "It is finished" with a clear conscience.

Of Harry Truman, Dean Acheson has written, "His ego never came between him and his job. He saw his job and its needs without distortion from that astigmatism."*

It is not easy so to separate ourselves from our work; it is hard to believe that we are not indispensable, perhaps not needed for the particular tasks upon which we are engaged. Obviously there are times when we should stick

---

* Dean Acheson, *Present at the Creation* (New York: W.W. Norton and Company, Inc., 1969), pp. 732-33.

to what we are doing, yet it is very dangerous to assume that the work would fail if we left it. The poor in spirit are blessed in their knowledge that the kingdom is more important than themselves and that in the building of the kingdom their work will count.

There is always something pathetic about the leaving of an important work or the closing of a great career, no matter how complete the work or the career seems to have been. I have never forgotten a remark a friend made after the death of William Temple, Archbishop of Canterbury, in 1944, when his wisdom and leadership seemed so sorely needed in the postwar world. "Perhaps when we come to lean too much on any one person God allows him to go in order that we may learn to stand together in God's strength."

There are times when even God seems to say "It is finished." According to the creation story he fashioned all the universe in six days and rested on the seventh. This cannot be an historical description and science finds no pause in creation, only ceaseless activity and change. Still, the old story contains truth for God does leave much of the work he has done in human hands to develop or to destroy, to beautify or to corrupt. He refuses to manipulate men and their history, no matter how tragic or noble such history may be without his hand in it or his signature on it. This is the meaning of our freedom, and perhaps not ours alone, for freedom may well be built into the very structure of the universe, even down to the cell and the atom. Like his son, God can go away and let others carry on his work, accepting the consequences of their choices. Apparently God does not consider himself indispensible in all circumstances nor does he allow his ego to get between himself and his job.

It was Jesus, poor in goods, poor in spirit, comparing entrance into the kingdom of God to the open, eager trust of a child, who said: "It is finished." To the degree we follow him we need not fear that our work, too, can be finished.

# VIII

## PURITY

## THROUGH PURGATION

St. Luke 23:46    *"Then, Jesus crying with a loud voice, said, 'Father, into thy hands I commit my spirit!' And having said this, he breathed his last." (R.S.V.)*

St. Matthew 5:8    *"Blessed are the pure in heart, for they shall see God." (R.S.V.)*

NO MAN but Christ could promise with such assurance that the pure in heart should see God. He lived that way and he died that way. Because all along his heart had burned with a consuming desire to do the will of God he could say with confidence at the end, "Father, into thy hands I commend my spirit." In this saying was gathered up the meaning of his whole life. It suggests the title of Jeremy Taylor's famous book *Holy Living and Holy Dying,* for on the cross holy living became holy dying.

Like one of the other phrases on the cross this one is taken from the Psalms. Psalm 31 has a verse reading, "Into thy hand I commit my spirit, thou hast redeemed me, O Lord, faithful God." No man ever took an ancient classic and prefixed to it "Father" with more right than did Jesus. He has shared that right with all of his followers. Saint Paul puts it in his Epistle to the Galatians, "To prove that you are sons, God has sent into our hearts the Spirit of his Son, crying 'Abba! Father!' "

As Christ has shared that right with all his followers he would extend the recognition of sonship to every person on earth. For all men are children of God. This was charmingly illustrated in a conversation between a seven-year-old boy and his teacher in a parochial school. This boy was the only member of his class who was not baptized and the teacher was trying to persuade him to agree to be.

"Why should I?" he kept asking.

"Well, it will make you a child of God," said the teacher, not quite knowing what else to say.

"I thought I always was."

Indeed all people are children of God, simply for having been created by him. Yet the recognition of that sonship comes with unique and particular force through the assurance and example of Christ. Taught by him and looking at him we have the greater boldness to say, "Our Father—"

Only the pure in heart know the depth and the fullness of speaking to God in this way. Pureness of heart does not mean avoidance of the world or retreat from the flesh. It is not a means of protection from the dirt of the world, for Christ could touch dirt without being defiled by it. It does not mean turning away from the needs of man to the contemplation of God, save as times of contemplation clarify our vision and our thinking, sending us back to be all the more involved in the service of others. Pureness of heart is the lifting of all life to the purging, the cleansing, and the enobling glory of God.

Our greatest personal disasters can be traced to the lack of purity of heart that shuts out the reality of God. Our minds and lives then become cluttered and corrupted with meaningless activities, with resentments, hatreds, and frustration.

Herein also lies the greatest failure of the Church. One hears the Church faulted on many grounds. The work and the life of any congregation are sure to be severely criticized, sometimes in ignorance and with unfairness, sometimes with cutting accuracy. We are accused of being timid, irrelevant, self-serving, out of touch with the real needs of people. All these things may often be true, but the surprising fact is that one rarely hears the reason why they are true or is confronted with the criticism more tragically just than all the others: that we who make up the Church lack the purity of heart, lack the singleness of aim, to see the reality of God with sufficient clarity, to listen to the voice of God in his concern for our world, and to reflect the glory of God so that others may see it on our faces and in our manner of living, in our commitment, in our outreach and in our joy.

These words of Jesus about the pure of heart seeing God are in striking contrast to what God told Moses on Mount Sinai. After Moses had prayed, "Show me thy glory," God answered, "You cannot see my face, for man shall not see me and live." Then God put Moses in the cleft of a rock and covered him with his hand until he had passed by. "Then I will take away my hand and you shall see my back; but my face shall not be seen." (Exodus 33:18–23 R.S.V.)

There is profound wisdom in this story, for human beings cannot take too much reality, certainly not all at once, and peoples' spirits can be destroyed by an overdose of truth for which they are not prepared, particularly truth about themselves. The trained pastor and the understanding friend will not succumb to the temptation to "level" with another wihout being sensitive to that person's readiness to know the whole truth about himself. There are dogs whose heads are so covered with hair that they see the world outside themselves very dimly; to cut off their hair all at once can produce blindness.

No man can look upon God and live, not as he lived before. To look upon God means to have the bright light of divine purity burn out the infections of our souls, in our cities and in our churches. As Paul saw so clearly, it is to be crucified with Christ that we may live again with him and that he may live in us. And we all face choices, sometimes very crucial choices, of whether we will crucify Christ in ourselves and in our relationships, or die with him. It was King David who is said to have sung after a great misadventure involving the murder of another man in order that he might have his wife, "Create in me a clean heart, O God, and put a new and right spirit within me. Fill me with joy and gladness; let the bones which thou hast broken rejoice." (Psalm 51:10,8 R.S.V.) David's shattered life was restored and in the end the wife whom he had taken became the mother of his son, Solomon, and an ancestress of Jesus Christ. From Jesus on the cross we derive the courage to look upon the face of God, confident that he will make within us a clean heart, so that even our broken bones may rejoice. I think of friends who have acquired wisdom and known fulfillment after turbulent and shattering experiences, whose faces bear the marks of pain and at the same time radiate joy.

True faith is purgative. Growth in grace is not a matter of learning more and more about what are sometimes called holy things, it is not crowding our time with prayers, and it is certainly not cultivating devout feelings. It is not even going about doing good, although good works are a result and a test of true faith. Such faith is allowing the fire of the Spirit to burn away the irrelevant dross, the long-time sloth, the uncritically accepted opinions, and the absorption with self. It involves a sharp simplification of life, simplification of goal amid complexity of circumstances, a serene simplification in the midst of turmoil and activity, in pain and in joy. It is never accomplished all at once and in trying to achieve it we frequently are overwhelmed by the responsibilities, the anxieties, and the temptations repeatedly met. We fall down and are picked up but strive on to the end when we say with our Lord, "Father, into thy hands I commend my spirit."

We are a rich nation and a privileged people; many of us belong to rich churches. We have our Lord's warning that it is not easy for people such as ourselves to enter the kingdom of God. One thinks of the rich young man, carrying his wealth off with him in defeat and into oblivion, and we know that but for the grace of God we will go the same way as did he. For our riches need not be money, although most of us possess a financial affluence that enables us to live better than kings did a fairly short time ago and makes us an island of comfort in a world of misery. Riches can also consist of health, or intelligence, or skill, or charm, or even virtue. Indeed. virtue can be a particularly dangerous kind of riches as is shown by the fact that the good people were not notably impressed by Jesus, but rather threatened by his friendship with outcasts and sinners. Purity of heart does not mean surrendering our virtues, but it may mean changing, burning, and breaking them until they become very different from what they are today.

It is very hard for the rich to enter the kingdom, yet incalculable are the treasures we can bring to that kingdom, to the entire world, if we become capable of offering them honestly and wisely and without the strings of our own pride. Riches offered by the pure in heart have for the first time in all history the capacity to lift the load of poverty and misery from the backs of men and to create a world of justice and freedom. Whether or not we are capable of offering them is another matter. Jesus himself said about the rich entering the kingdom, "With men it is impossible, but not with God; for all things are possible with God." And the story of the cross and the Resurrection is a story of impossibilities becoming realities.

May we, surfeited with many riches, find through death and resurrection the impossible paradox of detachment and abundance and discover the sharp thorny way and the strait gate to the kingdom of joy and peace.

Into thy hands we commend our spirits, now and forever, for thou hast redeemed us, O Lord, thou God of truth.